The Pappenheimers

An Animation and Vocabulary Guide

Tamara D. Stehr

Illustrated by Fred Garbers

Langenscheidt

New York · Berlin · München

To George and Corale Goesch, co-production partners in the rearing and education of the author.

Acknowledgements

Numerous individuals and organizations have contributed to the realization of the Pappenheimer project. It is only fitting to take this opportunity to express appreciation to some of the many whose efforts have brought the Pappenheimers "to life":

● Mr. Gerald Appy, Oregon Public Broadcasting, and his highly qualified staff

● Dr. Hans-Jürgen Daus, Westdeutscher Rundfunk, Cologne

● Dr. Helmut Müller and Mr. Bernd Nowald, Goethe Institute, Munich

● Dr. Ulrich Schaeffer, TransTel, Cologne

● Mr. Joachim Schönbeck, Auswärtiges Amt, Federal Republic of Germany

● Mr. Peter Lustig and Ms. Elfie Donnelly, West Berlin, authors of the original German television scripts

● Mr. Fred Garbers, Locomo Productions, New York, animator of the television series

Table of Contents

To the General Viewer

This "Animation and Vocabulary Guide" was written to accompany "The Pappenheimers", a television series designed to stimulate interest in and appreciation of German language and culture. The series was created with the broadest possible appeal in mind and for a wide spectrum of uses. This Guide is the first of several intended to accompany the series.

The Guide and the series are well suited to classroom use, as is pointed out in the Foreword to the Teacher, but the appeal does not stop there. General viewers of all ages and backgrounds will enjoy viewing "The Pappenheimers" and that enjoyment can be enhanced through this Guide.

The Guide is divided into two sections. The first section uses colorful illustrations to retell each of the 26 animated segments from the television series. The complete German dialogue from each cartoon is reproduced alongside the illustrations. A phonetic transcription and English translation are provided with each line of dialogue for easy reference.

The cartoons are recreated in word and picture for several reasons. They tie in with the themes of each of the real-life stories involving the Pappenheimer relatives and set in Germany. They also repeat the most important vocabulary items from those real-life scenes. This wealth of material thus allows the viewer to review at his/her leisure the basic contents of the television series. (In addition, an audio cassette of the animation dialogues is available from Langenscheidt, publisher of this Guide, thus making it possible for the viewer to review the sounds of German presented in the series also.) The adult viewer will find the animation section of the Guide a great stimulation, whether utilitizing for his/her own benefit, or working through it with a child.

The second section of the Guide is a comprehensive glossary of all German vocabulary used in the complete episodes of "The Pappenheimers". While the glossary is comprehensive and therefore will be of use even to those who are already acquainted with German, it is simple enough to use that non-German speakers will make good use of it also.

All of the vocabulary items in the glossary, including proper names, have been arranged strictly alphabetically. Nouns are alphabetized according to the spelling of the nouns themselves, ignoring the articles which precede them. [Every German noun is associated with an article of a specific gender; either masculine (der), feminine (die), or neuter (das), and these articles are listed with each noun in the glossary.] The inflected forms of some verbs are listed individually (particularly in those cases where the inflected forms vary greatly from the spelling of the infinitive), and those inflected forms are listed alphabetically rather than with the infinitive. Certain idiomatic expressions which are included are also listed alphabetically.

Every entry in the glossary is followed by a phonetic transcription to aid pronunciation. These phonetic transcriptions utilize the phonetic alphabet of the International Phonetic Association and are based on the phonetic transcriptions found in the leading German–English dictionaries published by Langenscheidt. Although the transcriptions may seem imposing at first, particulary if one has never had any exposure to a foreign language, a few minutes study of the Key to Pronunciation at the beginning of the glossary will provide even the novice with the information necessary to enable him/her to pronounce German words easily and correctly.

The English equivalents given for the German words found in the glossary correspond to the meanings used in the television series. Sometimes several equivalents are given; this is because sometimes the same German word occurs in several different contexts within the series. The viewer should simply try out the various possibilities until the appropriate meaning is found. By the same token, not all possible translations are given for every German word; many possible English equivalents simply don't apply to the contexts in which the German words occur in the series. In short, those English translations have been provided which correspond to the German usage in "The Pappenheimers".

Plural forms are given for al. German nouns in the glossary, although not all plurals are used in the series. These plural forms appear as endings listed in parentheses following the singular forms.

Since the dialogue in the series is virtually all in the present tense, past tense forms of verbs are deliberately avoided in the glossary.

It should be stressed that the glossary has been compiled to enhance the viewer's enjoyment of "The Pappenheimers". The glossary is there to help the viewer understand the German dialogue in the real-life film scenes and the animated segments; it is not there to teach the viewer German.

In conclusion, this Guide, like "The Pappenheimers" series itself, is intended to stimulate interest in and appreciation of German language and culture. No matter what the level of interest, or background in German, viewers should find it a useful and entertaining Guide.

As a final note, viewers are urged to take advantage of further guides planned to accompany "The Pappenheimers" television series. A culture and geography guide will expand on the material on those subjects presented in the real-life film scenes set in Germany. A song guide will contain music and lyrics for the songs presented by the host of "The Pappenheimers", Charley Pappenheimer.

To the Teacher

This "Animation and Vocabulary Guide" was written to accompany "The Pappenheimers", a television series designed to stimulate interest in and appreciation of German language and culture. The series was created with the broadest possible appeal in mind and for a wide spectrum of uses. This Guide is the first of several intended to facilitate utilization of the television series in the classroom.

The Guide consists of two main sections. The first section retells through colorful illustrations each of the 26 animated segments (cartoons) which appear in the television series. All German dialogue from the animated segments is reproduced alongside the illustrations, along with phonetic transcriptions and English translations.

The second section of the Guide consists of a comprehensive glossary of all German vocabulary used in the complete episodes of "The Pappenheimers".

The first section focuses on the animated segments for several reasons. Not only do the cartoons tie in with the themes of each of the real-life stories about the Pappenheimers set in Germany, but they also reinforce virtually all major vocabulary items from those real-life scenes. These cartoons serve as a very concise and manageable vehicle of reinforcement that has the added advantage of being highly stimulating and motivating.

The animated segments are recreated in this Guide because it may not always be feasible or desirable to view the complete television episodes in the classroom in order to review vocabulary or stimulate discussion about content. It is, however, easy to work on dialogues and enliven discussion through means of this Guide (preferably in conjunction with the use of a video cassette of the animation segments available from Oregon Public Broadcasting*, or an audio cassette of the dialogues available from the publisher of this Guide, Langenscheidt).

The possibilites for Pappenheimer classroom activities deriving from this Guide are endless. Students can focus on the illustrations and name the characters and objects. They can learn the German dialogues in their entirety and present miniplays, acting out the scenes from the cartoons. By covering the English translations, students can work out their own translations of the German dialogues; or they can cover the German dialogues and recreate them from the English translations. With the aid of the suggested video cassette or audio tape, students can work on their pronunciation skills. Students can create their own bilingual dictionaries encompassing the vocabulary from the animation dialogues. The colorful drawings in the Guide should inspire them to create their own illustrations for their dictionaries.

* Oregon Public Broadcasting Distribution Center
230 Kidder Hall
Oregon State University
Corvallis, OR 97331

The second section of the Guide, the glossary, is intended primarily for use by the teacher as well as more advanced students. As stated above, it contains all the vocabulary which occurs in "The Pappenheimers" television series.

All of the vocabulary items in the glossary, including proper names, have been arranged strictly alphabetically. Nouns are alphabetized according to the spelling of the nouns themselves, ignoring the articles which precede them. [Every German noun is associated with an article of a specific gender; either masculine (der), feminine (die), or neuter (das), and these articles are listed with each noun in the glossary.] The inflected forms of some verbs are listed individually (particularly in those cases where the inflected forms vary greatly from the spelling of the infinitive), and those inflected forms are listed alphabetically rather than with the infinitive. Certain idiomatic expressions which are included are also listed alphabetically.

Every entry in the glossary is followed by a phonetic transcription to aid pronunciation. These phonetic transcriptions utilize the phonetic alphabet of the International Phonetic Association and are based on the phonetic transcriptions found in the leading German–English dictionaries published by Langenscheidt, publishers of this Guide. Although the transcriptions may seem imposing at first, particularly if one has never had any exposure to a foreign language, a few minutes study of the Key to Pronunciation at the beginning of the glossary will provide even the novice with the information necessary to enable him/her to pronounce German words easily and correctly.

The English equivalents given for the German words found in the glossary correspond to the meanings used in the television series. Sometimes several equivalents are given; this is because sometimes the same German word occurs in several different contexts within the series. The user should simply try out the various English words until the appropriate meaning is found. By the same token, not all possible translations are given for every German word; many possible English equivalents simply don't apply to the contexts in which the German words occur in the series. In short, those English translations have been provided which correspond to the German usage within the series.

Plural forms are given for all German nouns in the glossary, although not all plurals are used in the series. These plural forms appear as endings listed in parentheses following the singular forms.

Since the dialogue in the series is virtually all in the present tense, past tense forms of verbs are deliberately avoided in the glossary, particularly since the past tense forms can be highly irregular in German.

In conclusion, the glossary is extensive enough in scope that even advanced students of German and German-speaking teachers will find it useful; yet it is simple enough to use that non-German speakers can make good use of it also.

Like "The Pappenheimers" television series itself, this Guide is intended to have a wide appeal. Classroom activities based on it can easily be adapted to the student's skill level as well as the teacher's needs. The television series and this Guide are suited for use in "Total Immersion" foreign language programs at the early levels and in so-called "Saturday Schools". They are just as well suited for use in "Foreign Language in the Elementary School" (FLES) and "Foreign Language Experience" (FLEX) programs at nearly all levels. They can be utilized by teachers with no background in German (this is not a language teaching program; it is a language and culture appreciation program) as well as those teachers who happen to be fluent.

As a final note, teachers are urged to utilize further guides planned to accompany "The Pappenheimers" television series. A culture and geography guide will expand on the material on those subjects presented in the real-life film scenes set in Germany. A song guide will contain music and lyrics for the songs presented by the host of "The Pappenheimers", Charley Pappenheimer.

"The Foot and the Fish"

FOOT SINGING

FISH: **Guten Tag!**
[guːtən ˈtɑːk]
Good day!

FOOT: **Guten Tag!**
[guːtən ˈtɑːk]
Good day!

FISH: **Ein Fuß?**
[aın ˈfuːs]
A foot?

FOOT: **Ein Fuß!**
[aın ˈfuːs]
A foot!

FISH: **Ein Fuß im Boot?**
[aın ˈfuːs im boːt]
A foot in the (a) boat?

FOOT: **Ein Fuß im Boot!**
[aın ˈfuːs im boːt]
A foot in the (a) boat!

FOOT: Ein Fisch? Im Wasser?
[aın 'fiʃ] [im 'vasər]
A fish? In the water?

FISH: Ein Fisch im Wasser!
[aın 'fiʃ im 'vasər]
A fish in the water!

FOOT SINGING AGAIN

FOOT: He, mein Boot!
[he: maın 'bo:t]
Hey, my boat!

11

FOOT: Mein Boot ist kaputt!
[maɪn 'boːt ist ka'put]
My boat is broken!

FOOT SINGING AGAIN

FISH: Au! He, Fuß!
[aʊ] [heːˈfuːs]
Ow! Hey, foot!

FISH & FOOT SINGING TOGETHER

"The Knight"

KNIGHT:

Au!
[aʊ]
Ow!

Was ist das hier?
[vas ist 'das hiːr]
What is this here?

KNIGHT 2:

Das ist ein Ritter!
[das ist aın 'ritər]
This is a knight!

KNIGHT:

Oh! Guten Tag!
[oː] [guːtən 'taːk]
Oh! Good day!

KNIGHT: **Das ist mein Fuß!**
[das ist maın 'fuːs]
That is my foot!

KNIGHT 2: **Nein! Mein Fuß!**
['naın] ['maın fuːs]
No! My foot!

Das ist mein Fuß!
[das ist 'maın fuːs]
That is my foot!

KNIGHT: **Was ist das?**
[vas 'ist das]
What is that?

Oh! Das ist Wasser!
[oː] [das ist 'vasər]
Oh! That is water!

KNIGHT: **Was ist das?**
[vas 'ist das]
What is this?

FISH VENDOR: **Das hier?**
['das hiːr]
This here?

Das ist ein Fisch!
['das ist aɪn 'fiʃ]
This is a fish!

KNIGHT: **Ja, das ist ein Fisch!**
[jɑ] [das ist aɪn 'fiʃ]
Yes, that is a fish!

Guten Tag!
[guːtən 'tɑːk]
Good day!

DRAGON: **Was ist das?**
[vas 'ist das]
What is this?

KNIGHT: **Das ist ein Ritter.**
[das ist aɪn 'ritər]
This is a knight!

DRAGON: **Das hier ist kaputt!**
[das hiːr ist kaˈput]
This here is broken!

KNIGHT: **Nein, nein!**
[naɪn ˈnaɪn]
No, no!

DRAGON: **Ja! Das ist kaputt!**
[jɑː] [das ist kaˈput]
Yes! This is broken!

KNIGHT: **Danke schön!**
[ˈdaŋkə ʃøːn]
Thank you!

DRAGON: **Bitte schön!**
[ˈbitə ʃøːn]
You're welcome!

17

"Tuba, Cow, and Tourist"

TUBA: Guten Tag! Ich bin . . . Ich bin . . .
[guːtən 'taːk] [iç 'bin . . . iç 'bin]
Good day! I am . . . I am . . .

Ich bin . . .
[iç 'bin]
I am . . .

COW: Eine Tuba!
['aɪnə 'tuːba]
A tuba!

TUBA: Danke!
['daŋkə]
Thanks!

COW: Bitte!
['bitə]
You're welcome!

TUBA: **Ich bin eine Tuba.**
[iç bin 'ainə 'tu:ba]
I am a tuba.

COW: **Ich bin eine Kuh!**
[iç bin 'ainə 'ku:]
I am a cow!

TUBA: **Eins, zwei, drei!**
['ains 'tsvai 'drai]
One, two, three!

COW & TUBA SINGING WITH THE MUSIC

19

TOURIST: Guten Tag! Ich bin Tourist!
[guːtən 'tɑːk] [iç bin tu'rist]
Good day! I am (a) tourist!

TUBA: Ich bin . . . ah . . . ich bin . . .
[iç 'bin . . . ɑː . . . iç 'bin]
I am . . . ah . . . I am . . .

COW: Eine Tuba!
['aɪnə 'tuːba]
A tuba!

TOURIST: Eine Tuba?
['aɪnə 'tuːba]
A tuba?

COW: Nein! Eine Kuh!
[naɪn] ['aɪnə kuː]
No! A cow!

Muh!
['muː]
Moo!

21

"The Little Cow"

COW WHISTLING

BOY: Was ist das?
[vas 'ist das]
What is that?

GIRL: Das ist eine Kuh!
['das ist aɪnə 'kuː]
That is a cow!

BOY: Eine braune Kuh!
['aɪnə 'braʊnə 'kuː]
A brown cow!

COW: Guten Tag!
[guːtən 'taːk]
Good day!

GIRL: Guten Tag, Kuh!
[guːtən 'taːk 'kuː]
Good day, cow!

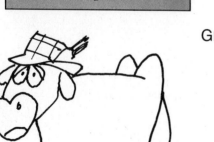

COW: Ich bin Tourist! Ich habe Hunger!
[iç bin tu'rist] [iç 'haːbə 'huŋər]
I am (a) tourist! I am hungry! (lit: I have hunger!)

Muh!
[muː]
Moo!

GIRL: Hier ist Salat!
[hiːr ist za'lɑt]
Here ist lettuce!

BOY: Die Kuh ist grün!
[diː kuː ist 'gryːn]
The cow is green!

GIRL: Der Salat ist grün, und die Kuh ist grün.
[deːr za'lɑt ist 'gryːn unt diː 'kuː ist gryːn]
The lettuce is green and the cow is green.

GIRL: Nein, braun . . .
[naɪn ˈbraʊn]
No, brown . . .

BOY: Nein, grün . . .
[naɪn ˈɡryːn]
No, green . . .

COW: Gut, guuuuuut! Hier ist Milch!
[ɡuːt ɡuːt] [hiːr ist ˈmilç]
Good, gooooood! Here is milk!

GIRL: Eins, zwei, eins, zwei . . .
[ˈaɪns tsvaɪ ˈaɪns tsvaɪ]
One, two, one, two . . .

BOY: **Die Milch ist gut!**
[di: milç ist ˈguːt]
The milk is good!

Danke!
[ˈdaŋkə]
Thanks!

COW: **Bitte!**
[ˈbitə]
You're welcome!

COW WHISTLING

25

"The Wet Guest"

GUEST: Herr Ober!
[hɛr 'o:bər]
Waiter!

Herr Ober!
[hɛr 'o:bər]
Waiter!

Ich möchte Kaffee!
[iç 'mœçtə 'kafe]
I would like coffee!

GUEST: **Ich möchte Zucker!**

[iç ˈmœçtə ˈtsukər]

I would like sugar!

GUEST: **Ich möchte Milch!**
[iç 'mœçtə 'milç]
I would like milk!

Was ist das?
[vas 'ist das]
What is this?

Herr Ober!
[hɛr 'oːbər]
Waiter!

GUEST: Was kostet das?

[vas 'kɔstət das]
What does this cost?
(lit: What costs this?)

WAITER: Das kostet eine Mark!

[das 'kɔstət 'aɪnə mark]
That costs one mark!

GUEST: Eine Mark sind hundert Pfennige!

[aɪnə 'mark zint 'hundərt 'pfɛnigə]
One mark is (a) hundred pennies!

"Pirates in a Bottle"

CAPTAIN: Ich möchte ein Schiff! Ein Schiff!
[iç ˈmœçtə aɪn ˈʃif] [aɪn ˈʃif]
I would like a ship! A ship!

PIRATE: Eine Mark . . . Ein Pfennig . . . Eine Mark . . . Ein Pfennig . . . Eine Mark . . .

[aɪnə ˈmark aɪn ˈpfɛnɪç aɪnə ˈmark aɪn ˈpfɛnɪç aɪnə ˈmark]
One mark . . . one penny . . . one mark . . . one penny . . . one mark . . .

LOOKOUT: Ein Schiff!
[aɪn ˈʃif]
A ship!

PIRATE: **Ein Schiff?**
[aɪn ˈʃif]
A ship?

CAPTAIN: **Ein Schiff? Gut!**
[aɪn ˈʃif] [guːt]
A ship? Good!

LOOKOUT: **Nein! Eine Flasche!**
[naɪn] [ˈaɪnə ˈflaʃə]
No! A bottle!

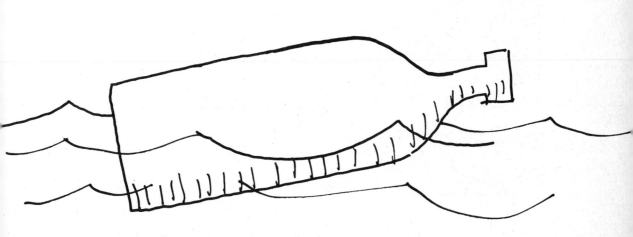

PIRATE: **Eine Flasche?**
['aɪnə 'flaʃə]
A bottle?

CAPTAIN: **Eine Flasche?**
['aɪnə 'flaʃə]
A bottle?

PIRATE: **Eine Mark . . . ein Pfennig . . . eine Mark . . .**
[aɪnə 'mark aɪn 'pfɛnɪç aɪnə 'mark]
A mark . . . a penny . . . a mark . . .

LOOKOUT: **Eine große Flasche!**
[aɪnə 'groːsə 'flaʃə]
A big bottle!

CAPTAIN &
PIRATE:

Oh! Eine große Flasche!
[oː] [ˈaɪnə ˈɡroːsə ˈflaʃə]
Oh! A big bottle!

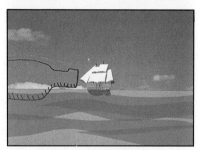

Nein! Nein!
[naɪn] [naɪn]
No! No!

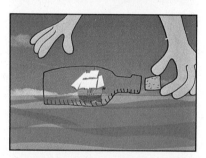

"The Assembly Line"

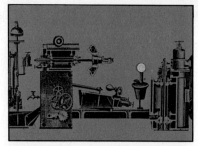

MAN: Ich habe Hunger!

[iç ˈhɑːbə ˈhuŋər]
I am hungry! (lit: I have hunger!)

ROBOT: Das ist verboten!

[das ist fɛrˈboːtən]
That is forbidden!

MAN: Hatschi!

[haˈtʃiː]
Ah-choo!

ROBOT: **Gesundheit!**
[ge'zunthaɪt]
Bless you!

MAN: **Danke!**
['daŋkə]
Thanks!

MAN: **Hatschi!**
[ha'tʃiː]
Ah-choo!

ROBOT: **Verboten!**
[fɛr'boːtən]
Forbidden!

MAN: Das ist schnell! Das ist zu schnell!
[das ist ˈʃnɛl] [das ist ˈtsu ʃnɛl]
That is fast! That is too fast!

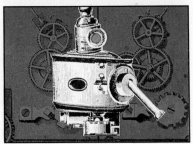

ROBOT: Nein, es ist gut! Ich bin ein Roboter! Ich bin schnell!
[naɪn ɛs ist ˈguːt] [iç bin aɪn ˈroːbɔtər] [iç bin ˈʃnɛl]
No, it is good! I am a robot! I am fast!

Ich bin ein Roboter! Ich bin schnell!
[iç bin aɪn ˈroːbɔtər] [iç bin ˈʃnɛl]
I am a roboter! I am fast!

ROBOT: Ich bin ein Roboter! Ich bin schnell!
[iç bin aın ˈroːbɔtər] [iç bin ˈʃnɛl]
I am a robot! I am fast!

MAN: He! Das ist verboten!
[heː] [das ist fɛrˈboːtən]
That is forbidden!

Das ist . . .
[das ist]
That is . . .

"The Sheep and the Dog"

DOG: Guten Tag, Schaf!
[guːtən ˈtɑːk ˈʃɑːf]
Good day, sheep!

SHEEP: Guten Tag, Schaf!
[guːtən ˈtɑːk ˈʃɑːf]
Good day, sheep!

DOG: Ich bin kein Schaf! Ich bin ein Hund!
[iç ˈbin kaɪn ˈʃɑːf] [iç bin aɪn ˈhunt]
I am not a seal! No, I am a dog!

SHEEP: Oh! Guten Tag, Hund!
[oː] [guːtən ˈtɑːk ˈhunt]
Oh! Good day, dog!

SHEEP: Hier! Das ist ein Meter!
[hiːr] [das ist aın 'meːtər]
Here! This is a meter!

DOG: Hier! Zwei Meter! Schön weiß!
[hiːr] [tsvaı 'meːtər] [ʃøːn vaıs]
Here! Two meters! Pretty white!

SHEEP: Da! Drei Meter!
[dɑː] [draı 'meːtər]
There! Three meters!

DOG: Vier Meter! Schön weiß!
[fiːr 'meːtər] [ʃøːn vaɪs]
Four meters! Pretty white!

SHEEP: Nein . . . braun!
[naɪn 'braʊn]
No . . . brown!

Es ist braun!
[ɛs ist 'braʊn]
It is brown!

SHEEP: Braun? Braun!
['braʊn] ['braʊn]
Brown? Brown!

Oh! Das ist nicht gut!
[oː] [das ist 'nɪçt guːt]
Oh! That is not good!

DOG: Hier! Das ist für dich!
[hiːr] [das ist fyːr 'dɪç]
Here! This is for you!

SHEEP: Für mich?
[fyːr 'mɪç]
For me?

Oh! Danke, Hund!
[oː] ['daŋkə hunt]
Oh! Thanks, dog!

"The Dog Who Wanted to be a Seal"

DOG: Hallo! Ich bin ein Seehund!
[ha'lo:] [iç bin aɪn 'ze:hunt]
Hello! I am a seal!

SEAL: Ein Seehund!
[aɪn 'ze:hunt]
A seal!

DOG: Ja, ich bin ein Seehund!
[jɑː iç bin aɪn 'ze:hunt]
Yes, I am a seal!

Eine See . . .
[aɪnə 'ze:]
A sea . . .

. . . ein Hund!
[aɪn 'hunt]
a dog!

Ein Seehund!
[aɪn ˈzeːhunt]
A seal!

Das Wasser ist weg!
[das ˈvasər ist vɛk]
The water is gone!

Es ist sieben Uhr . . .
[ɛs ist ˈziːbən uːr]
It is seven o'clock . . .

Wo ist das Wasser?
[voː ist das ˈvasər]
Where is the water?

Oh! Da ist das Wasser!
[oː] [ˈdɑː ist das ˈvasər]
Oh! There is the water!

SEAL: **Der Seehund!**
[deːr ˈzeːhunt]
The seal!

DOG: Ich bin kein Seehund! Nein, ich bin ein Hund!

[iç 'bin kaın 'zeːhunt] [naın iç bin aın 'hunt]

I am not a seal! No, I am a dog!

Danke! Du bist mein Freund!

['daŋkə] [duː bist maın 'frɔynt]

Thanks! You are my friend!

He!

[he]

Hey!

SEAL: Ein frischer Fisch!

[aın 'friʃər fiʃ]

A fresh fish!

DOG: Ich möchte keinen Fisch!

[iç 'mœçtə kaınən fiʃ]

I would not like a fish!

"Pirates in a Fish"

CAPTAIN: Da! Nach Norden! Schnell!
[dɑː] [nɑːx ˈnɔrdən] [ʃnɛl]
There! To (the) north! Quickly!

HELMSMAN: Nein, das ist Norden!
[naɪn ˈdas ist ˈnɔrdən]
No, that is north!

Da ist Westen!
[dɑː ist ˈvestən]
There is west!

PIRATE: Eins, zwei, drei-hundert . . .
[aɪns tsvaɪ draɪ ˈhundərt]
One, two, three-hundred . . .

Norden ist links!
[ˈnɔrdən ist lɪŋks]
North is left!

Eins, zwei, drei-hundert . . .
[aɪns tsvaɪ draɪ ˈhundərt]
One, two, three-hundred . . .

CAPTAIN: **Nein! Norden ist rechts!**
[naɪn] ['nɔrdən ist rɛçts]
No! North is right!

Wo ist der Kompaß?
[voː ist deːr 'kɔmpas]
Where is the compass?

MECHANIC: **Der Kompaß ist kaputt!**
[deːr 'kɔmpas ist ka'put]
The compass is broken!

CAPTAIN: **Wo ist Norden?**
[voː ist 'nɔrdən]
Where is north?

LOOKOUT: **Da! Das ist . . .**
[daː] [das ist]
There! That is . . .

CAPTAIN: **Norden?**
['nɔrdən]
North?

LOOKOUT: Nein! Ein Fisch! Ich sehe einen Fisch!

[naɪn] [aɪn ˈfiʃ] [iç ˈzeːə aɪnən ˈfiʃ]
No! A fish! I see a fish!

CAPTAIN, HELMSMAN & PIRATE: Ein Fisch?

[aɪn ˈfiʃ]
A fish?

ALL INSIDE FISH: Ein Fisch? Wo ist Norden? Links? Nein rechts! Hier ist kein Licht! Ich möchte nach Hause!

[aɪn ˈfiʃ] [voː ist ˈnɔrdən] [liŋks]
[naɪn ˈrɛçts] [hiːr ist kaɪn ˈliçt]
[iç ˈmœçtə naːx ˈhaʊsə]
A fish? Where is north? Left?
No right! Here is no light!
I would like to go home!

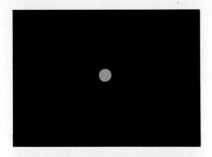

Da! Ein Stern! Nein!
Das ist ein Licht! Schnell!
Das ist Wilhelm Pappenheimer!

[dɑː] [aɪn ˈʃtɛrn] [naɪn]
[das ist aɪn ˈlɪçt] [ʃnɛl]
[das ist ˈvilhɛlm ˈpapənhaɪmər]
There! A star! No!
That is a light! Quickly!
That is Wilhelm Pappenheimer!

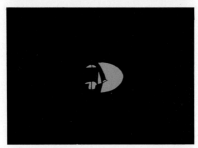

Das ist Wilhelm Pappenheimer!

[das ist ˈvilhɛlm ˈpapənhaɪmər]
That is Wilhelm Pappenheimer!

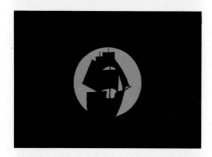

Das ist . . . nein! Das ist die See!
Wo ist Norden? Links! Nein rechts!
Ich möchte nach Hause!

[das ist] [naɪn] [das ist diː ˈzeː]
[voː ist ˈnɔrdən] [liŋks] [naɪn ˈrɛçts]
[iç ˈmœçtə naːx ˈhauzə]
That is . . . no! That is the sea!
Where is north? Left? No right!
I would like to go home!

"The Bear Photographer"

BEAR: **Was ist das?**
[vas 'ist das]
What is this?

Ist das kaputt?
[ist das ka'put]
Is this broken?

Aua! Hilfe!
['aʊa] ['hilfə]
Ow! Help!

BEAR: Ich sehe nichts!
[iç ˈzeːə niçts]
I see nothing!

Eins, zwei, drei, vier . . .
[aɪns tsvaɪ draɪ fiːr]
One, two, three, four . . .

Hier!
[hiːr]
Here!

BEAR: **Ein Foto, meine Damen und Herren!**
[aın 'foːto maınə 'daːmən unt 'hɛrən]
A photo, ladies and gentlemen!

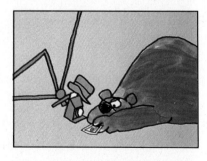

Ein Foto!
[aın 'foːto]
A photo!

BEAR: Hier! Mit Bär!

[hiːr] [mit 'bɛːr]
Here! With (a) bear!

VOICE OF HAND: Meine Damen und Herren! Hier!

[maɪnə 'dɑːmən unt 'hɛrən] [hiːr]
Ladies and gentlemen! Here!

Ein Foto mit Bär!

[aɪn 'foːto mit 'bɛr]
A photo with (a) bear!

Ein Foto kostet fünf Mark!

[aɪn 'foːto kɔstət 'fynf 'mark]
A photo costs five marks!

"Clowning around"

BIG CLOWN: Meine Damen und Herren!
[maɪnə ˈdɑːmən unt ˈhɛrən]
Ladies and gentlemen!

Ich bin . . .
[iç bin]
I am . . .

LITTLE CLOWN: Halt!
[halt]
Stop!

Die Kinder!
[diː ˈkɪndər]
The children!

BIG CLOWN: Kinder? Kinder?
[ˈkɪndər] [ˈkɪndər]
Children? Children?

BIG CLOWN: Wo?
['voː]
Where?

LITTLE CLOWN: Da!
['dɑː]
There!

BIG CLOWN: Oh! Guten Tag, Kinder!
[oː] [guːtən 'tɑːk 'kindər]
Oh! Good day, children!

Ich bin ein Clown!
[iç bin aɪn 'klaʊn]
I am a clown!

LITTLE CLOWN: Halt!
[halt]
Stop!

LITTLE CLOWN: **Ich möchte Musik!**
[iç ˈmœçtə muˈziːk]
I would like (some) music!

Hier ist eine Gitarre!
[hiːr ist ˈaɪnə giˈtarə]
Here is a guitar!

BIG CLOWN: **Das ist eine Gitarre?**
[das ist ˈaɪnə giˈtarə]
That is a guitar?

LITTLE CLOWN: **Ja! Eine schöne Gitarre!**
[jaː] [ˈaɪnə ˈʃøːnə giˈtarə]
Yes! A nice guitar!

BIG CLOWN: **Nein! Das ist ein Würstchen!**
[naɪn] [das ist aɪn ˈvyrstçen]
No! That is a sausage!

LITTLE CLOWN: **Das ist eine Gitarre!**
[das ist ˈaɪnə giˈtarə]
This is a guitar!

GUITAR MUSIC

LITTLE CLOWN: **Bitte! Eine Gitarre!**
[ˈbitə] [ˈaɪnə giˈtarə]
(If you) please! A guitar!

BIG CLOWN: **Nein! Ein Würstchen!**
[naɪn] [aɪn ˈvyrstçən]
No! A sausage!

GUITAR MUSIC

57

"The Hungry Toaster"

TOASTER: Guten Appetit!
['guːtən apeˈtiːt]
Bon appétit!

Guten Appetit!
['guːtən apeˈtiːt]
Bon appétit!

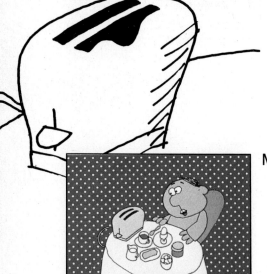

MAN: Oh! Guten Appetit!
[oː] ['guːtən apeˈtiːt]
Oh! Bon appétit!

MAN: He! Bist du kaputt?
[heː] [bist duː kaˈput]
Hey! Are you broken?

TOASTER: Nein! Ich habe Hunger!
[naɪn] [iç ˈhɑːbə ˈhuŋər]
No! I am hungry! (lit: I have hunger!)

Ich möchte ein Ei!
[iç ˈmœçtə aɪn ˈaɪ]
I would like an egg!

Danke!
[ˈdaŋkə]
Thanks!

Wo ist die Butter?
[voː ist diː ˈbutər]
Where is the butter?

MAN: Ich habe keine Butter!

[iç 'hɑːbə 'kaɪnə 'butər]

I have no butter!

TOASTER: Und was ist das?

[unt vas ist 'das]

And what is that?

MAN: Das ist meine Butter!

[das ist 'maɪnə 'butər]

That is my butter!

Und meine Marmelade!

[unt 'maɪnə marmə'lɑːdə]

And my jam!

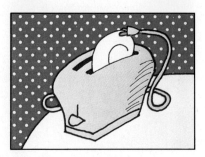

Mein Kaffee!

[maɪn 'kafe]

My coffee!

Meine Milch!

['maɪnə milç]

My milk!

60

MAN: **Mein Zucker!**
[maɪn ˈtsukər]
My sugar!

Halt!
[halt]
Stop!

TOASTER: **Ein gutes Frühstück!**
[aɪn ˈguːtəs ˈfryːʃtyk]
(That was) A good breakfast!

Guten Appetit!
[ˈguːtən apeˈtiːt]
Bon appétit!

"The Musicians"

APPLAUSE

SINGER: Meine Damen und Herren . . .
[maɪnə ˈdɑːmən unt ˈhɛrən]
Ladies and gentlemen . . .

Ruhe bitte! Ich mache Musik!
[ˈruːə ˈbitə] [iç maxə muˈziːk]
Quiet please! I (will) make music!

PIANIST: Nein! Ich mache Musik!
[naɪn] [ˈiç maxə muˈziːk]
No! I (will) make music!

SINGER: Gut, gut.
[ˈguːt ˈguːt]
Fine, fine.

SINGER: Eins, zwei, drei!
['aɪns 'tsvaɪ 'draɪ]
One, two, three!

Zum Geburtstag . . .
[tsum gə'buːrtstɑːk]
Happy birthday . . .
(lit: To the birthday . . .)

FLUTE MUSIC FROM THE PIANO

SINGER: Eins, zwei, drei! Zum Geburtstag . . .
['aɪns 'tsvaɪ 'draɪ] [tsum gə'buːrtstɑːk]
One, two, three! Happy birthday . . .

DRUMS FROM THE PIANO

SINGER: Eins, zwei, drei! Zum Geburtstag . . .

['aɪns 'tsvaɪ 'draɪ] [tsum gə'buːrtstɑːk]

One, two, three! Happy birthday . . .

DOG BARKING FROM THE PIANO

PIANIST: Was ist das?

[vas 'ist das]

What is this?

Ich höre eine Flöte, einen Hund, ein . . .

[iç 'høːrə aɪnə 'fløːtə aɪnən hunt aɪn]

I hear a flute, a dog, a . . .

SINGER: Das ist . . .

[das ist]

That is . . .

64

SINGER: **Ein Recorder! Da!**
[aɪn reˈkɔrdər] [dɑː]
A recorder (cassette player)! There!

PIANIST: **Ein Recorder? Hier?**
[aɪn reˈkɔrdər] [hiːr]
A recorder? Here?

SINGER: **Ja . . .**
[jɑː]
Yes . . .

DOG PLAYING DRUMS AND FLUTE

65

"The Christmas Bottle"

BOTTLE: Du bist schön!
[du: bist ˈʃøːn]
You are pretty!

ORNAMENT: Ja, ich bin schön!
[jɑː iç bin ˈʃøːn]
Yes, I am pretty!

BOTTLE: Ist das Glas?
[ist das ˈɡlɑːs]
Is that glass?

ORNAMENT: Ja, das ist Glas. Schönes Glas für Weihnachten!

[jɑː das ist ˈglɑːs] [ʃøːnəs ˈglɑːs fyːr ˈvaɪnaxtən]

Yes, this is glass. Pretty glass for Christmas!

BOTTLE: Oh, für Weihnachten. Das will ich auch!

[oː fyːr ˈvaɪnaxtən] [das vil iç ˈaux]

Oh, for Christmas. I want that (to be for Christmas) also!

ORNAMENT: Nein! Du bist eine Flasche!

[naɪn] [du bist ˈaɪnə ˈflaʃə]

No! You are a bottle!

Du bist nicht schön!

[duː bɪst ˈniçt ʃøːn]

You are not pretty!

BOTTLE GROANS WITH EXERTION

ORNAMENT LAUGHS AT THE BOTTLE

ORNAMENT:　Nein, du bist nicht schön!
[naɪn duː bist ˈnɪçt ʃøːn]
No, you are not pretty!

Du bist eine komische Flasche!
[duː bist ˈaɪnə ˈkoːmiʃə ˈflaʃə]
You are a funny bottle!

ORNAMENT LAUGHS AND CRACKS

BOTTLE LAUGHS AND LEAVES WHISTLING

MOUSE:

Ich bin eine Maus!
[iç bin aɪnə ˈmaʊs]
I am a mouse!

Und ich will nach oben!
[unt iç vil nɑːx ˈoːbən]
And I want (to go) to the top!

MOUSE:
Oh! Der Baum!
[oː] [deːr ˈbaʊm]
Oh! The tree!

Der Weihnachtsbaum!
[deːr ˈvaɪnaxtsbaʊm]
The Christmas tree!

Oh! Das bin ich!
[oː] [das bin iç]
Oh! That is I!

Ich bin schön!
[iç bin ˈʃøːn]
I am beautiful!

GINGERBREAD
HEART:
Ich bin am schönsten!
[iç bin am ˈʃøːnstən]
I am the most beautiful!

71

GINGERBREAD HEART: Ich bin ein Lebkuchen. Und du?
[iç bin aın 'leːpkuːxən] [unt 'duː]
I am (a) gingerbread. And you?

MOUSE: Ich bin eine Maus! Ich will nach oben!
[iç bin 'aınə maus] [iç vil naːx 'oːbən]
I am a mouse! I want (to go) to the top!

GINGERBREAD HEART: Was willst du oben?
[vas vilst duː 'oːbən]
What do you want at the top?

MOUSE: Oben mache ich Musik! Ich bin eine Weihnachtsmaus!
['oːbən 'maxə iç muˈziːk] [iç bin 'aınə 'vaınaxtsmaus]
At the top I (will) make music! I am a Christmas mouse!

Und, ich habe Hunger!
[unt iç 'haːbə 'huŋər]
And, I am hungry! (lit: I have hunger!)

MOUSE:　Au! Das ist heiß! Hilfe!
[aʊ] [das ist 'haɪs] ['hilfə]
Ow! That is hot! Help!

Ich bin oben! Ich bin eine Weihnachtsmaus!
[iç bin 'oːbən] [iç bin aɪnə 'vaɪnaxtsmaʊs]
I am at the top! I am a Christmas mouse!

MOUSE SINGS:　Oh du fröhliche, oh du selige . . .
[oː duː 'frøːliçə oː duː 'zeːligə]
Oh you joyous, oh you blessed . . .

"The Wasp in the Torte"

WASP: Hilfe! Hilfe!
['hilfə] ['hilfə]
Help! Help!

Hier! Hier bin ich!
[hiːr] ['hiːr bin iç]
Here! Here I am!

Es ist kalt!
[ɛs ist 'kalt]
It is cold!

WASP: Ist das Schnee? Ja, das ist Schnee!

[ist das 'ʃneː] [jɑː das ist 'ʃneː]

Is this snow? Yes, this is snow!

Und wo bin ich?

[unt voː bin 'iç]

And where am I?

Ich weiß nicht!

[iç 'vais niçt]

I don't know!

So viel Schnee!

['zoː fiːl ʃneː]

So much snow!

Ich muß skilaufen!

[iç mus 'ʃiːlaʊfən]

I must ski!

WASP: Ich laufe Ski! Nach unten!
[iç 'laʊfə ʃiː] [naːx 'untən]
I (will) ski! To the bottom!

Ich kann es nicht!
[iç 'kan ɛs niçt]
I cannot do it!

So! Nochmal!
[zoː] ['nɔxmaːl]
So! One more time!

Juchuu! Ich kann es!
[jux'hʊ] [iç 'kan ɛs]
Whoopee! I can (do) it!

Ich kann es!
[iç 'kan ɛs]
I can (do) it!

WASP: **Oh! Was ist das?**
[oː] [vas ˈist das]
Oh! What is this?

COCOA
OWNER: **Was ist das?**
[vas ˈist das]
What is this?

In meinem Kakao?
[in ˈmaɪnəm kaˈkaːo]
In my cocoa?

WASP: **Ich bin es!**
[ˈiç bin ɛs]
It is I!

Ich kann es!
[iç ˈkan ɛs]
I can (do) it!

Ich kann skilaufen!
[iç kan ˈʃilaʊfən]
I can ski!

"The Snowman at Carnival Time"

COW: **Hallo, Schneemann!**
[ha'lo: 'ʃneːman]
Hello, snowman!

SNOWMAN: **Hallo, Kuh!**
[ha'lo: 'kuː]
Hello, cow!

COW: **Heute ist Fasching!**
['hɔytə ist 'faʃiŋ]
Today is carnival!

SNOWMAN: **Fasching? Heute?**
['faʃiŋ] ['hɔytə]
Carnival? Today?

COW: **Ja! Komm mit!**
[jɑː] [kɔm 'mit]
Yes! Come along!

SNOWMAN: **Ich kann nicht!**
[iç 'kan niçt]
I cannot!

COW: Nein, du kannst nicht!

[naɪn duː ˈkanst nɪçt]
No, you cannot!

Auf Wiedersehen, Schneemann!

[aʊf ˈviːdərzeːən ˈʃneːman]
Good-bye, snowman!

RABBIT: Guten Tag, Schneemann!

[guːtən ˈtɑːk ˈʃneːman]
Good day, snowman!

Heute ist Fasching! Komm mit!

[ˈhɔytə ist ˈfaʃiŋ] [kɔm ˈmit]
Today is carnival! Come along!

SNOWMAN: Ich kann nicht!

[iç ˈkan nɪçt]
I cannot!

RABBIT: Nein, du kannst nicht!

[naɪn duː ˈkanst nɪçt]
No, you cannot!

BEAVERS: Guten Tag, Schneemann! Wie geht's?

[guːtən ˈtɑːk ˈʃneːman] [viˈɡeːts]

Good day, snowman! How are you?
(lit. How goes it?)

SNOWMAN: Schlecht! Mir geht's schlecht!

[ʃlɛçt] [miːr ɡeːts ˈʃlɛçt]

Terrible! I'm terrible! (lit: Me goes it terrible!)

Ich kann nicht zum Fasching!

[iç kan niçt tsum ˈfaʃiŋ]

I cannot (go) to carnival!

BEAVERS CONFER IN WHISPERS

BEAVERS: Paß auf!

[ˈpas aʊf]

Watch this! (lit: Watch out!)

SNOWMAN: **Was ist das?**
[vas ˈist das]
What is that?

BEAVERS: **Das sind Skier!**
[das zint ˈʃiːər]
Those are skis!

Du mußt skilaufen!
[du must ˈʃiːlaʊfən]
You must ski!

SNOWMAN: **Ich? Jetzt?**
[iç] [jɛtst]
I? Now?

BEAVERS: **Ja! Jetzt!**
[jɑː] [jɛtst]
Yes! Now!

Zum Fasching!
[tsum ˈfaʃiŋ]
To carnival!

"The Little Airplane"

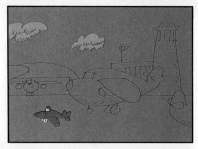

GLIDER: Ich . . . ich bin ein kleines Flugzeug!
[iç . . . iç bin aın 'klaınəs 'flu:ktsɔyk]
I . . . I am a little airplane!

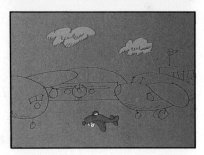

Ich habe keinen Motor!
[iç 'hɑ:bə 'kaınən 'mo:tɔr]
I have no engine!

JET: Du brauchst keinen Motor!
[du: 'braʊxst kaınən 'mo:tɔr]
You need no engine!

GLIDER: Wie heißt du?
[vi: 'haıst du:]
What's your name?
(lit: How are you called?)

JET: Ich bin das Flugzeug Nummer sechs, eins, zwei aus Bremen.

[iç bin das ˈfluːktsɔyk numər ˈzɛks ˈaɪns ˈtsvaɪ aʊs ˈbreːmən]

I am the plane number six, one, two from Bremen.

GLIDER: Ich möchte auch eine Nummer!

[iç ˈmœçtə ˈaʊx aɪnə ˈnumər]

I would also like a number!

Und ich möchte auch einen Motor!

[unt iç ˈmœçtə ˈaʊx aɪnən ˈmoːtɔr]

And I would also like an engine!

Ich möchte fliegen!

[iç ˈmœçtə ˈfliːgən]

I would like to fly!

JET: Komm, ich helfe dir!

[ˈkɔm iç ˈhɛlfə diːr]

Come, I (will) help you!

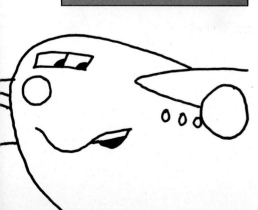

Du mußt jetzt fliegen!

[duː must jɛtst ˈfliːgən]

You must fly now!

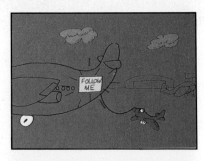

JET: Hinterherfliegen!
[hintər'heːrfliːɡən]
Fly behind (me)!

GLIDER: Ich kann nicht fliegen!
[iç 'kan niçt 'fliːɡən]
I cannot fly!

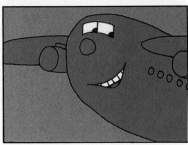

JET: Du kannst fliegen!
[duː 'kanst 'fliːɡən]
You can fly!

GLIDER: Ich fliege! Ich fliege!
[iç 'fliːɡə] [iç 'fliːɡə]
I am flying! I am flying!

He! Hilfe! Ein Baum!
[heː] ['hilfə] [aın 'baʊm]
Hey! Help! A tree!

JET: Was ist los?

[vas ist ˈloːs]

What is wrong?

GLIDER: Ein Baum! Ein Baum!

[aɪn ˈbaʊm] [aɪn ˈbaʊm]

A tree! A tree!

JET: Hier! Du mußt das machen!

[ˈhiːr] [du must ˈdas maxən]

Here! You must do this!

GLIDER: Juchuu! Ich kann fliegen!

[juxˈhu] [iç kan ˈfliːgən]

Whoopee! I can fly!

Ich brauche keinen Motor! Juchuu!

[iç ˈbraʊxə kaɪnən ˈmoːtɔr] [juxˈhu]

I need no engine! Whoopee!

"The Weather Frog"

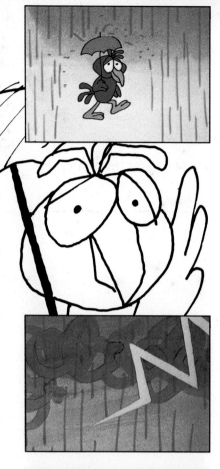

BIRD: **Das Wetter ist schlecht!**
[das ˈvɛtər ist ʃlɛçt]
The weather is terrible!

Ich kann nicht fliegen!
[iç kan niçt ˈfliːɡən]
I cannot fly!

Ich muß laufen!
[iç mus ˈlaʊfən]
I have to walk!

Was machst du hier?
[vas ˈmaxst duː hiːr]
What are you doing here?

FROG: Ich mache Wetter!

[iç 'maxə 'vɛtər]
I am making weather!

BIRD: Du kannst Wetter machen?

[du: kanst 'vɛtər 'maxən]
You can make weather?

FROG: Ja, ich kann! Paß auf!

[jɑ: iç 'kan] [pas 'aʊf]
Yes, I can! Watch this!
(lit: Watch out!)

BIRD: Oh! Das Wetter ist gut!

[oː] [das 'vɛtər ist 'guːt]
Oh! The weather is good!

FROG: **Paß auf!**
['pas auf]
Watch this! (lit: Watch out!)

BIRD: **Bravo! Die Wolken sind weg!**
['braːvo] [diː 'vɔlkən sint vɛk]
Bravo! The clouds are gone!

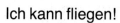

Ich kann fliegen!
[iç kan 'fliːgən]
I can fly!

BIRD: **Mach gutes Wetter! Bitte!**
[max 'guːtəs 'vɛtər] ['bitə]
Make good weather! Please!

FROG: **Nein!**
[naɪn]
No!

BIRD: Du mußt nach oben!
[du: must nɑːx ˈoːbən]
You must (go) to the top!

So! Der Himmel ist blau!
[zoː] [deːr ˈhiməl ist ˈblaʊ]
So! The sky is blue!

Jetzt kann ich fliegen!
[jɛtst kan iç ˈfliːgən]
Now I can fly!

"The Carrier Pigeon"

PIGEON: Guten Tag! Ich bin eine Taube!
[guːtən ˈtɑːk] [iç bin aɪnə ˈtaʊbə]
Good day! I am a pigeon!

Eine schöne, weiße Tau . . .
[ˈaɪnə ˈʃøːnə ˈvaɪsə ˈtaʊ]
A pretty, white pige . . .

Oh! Eine Hand!
[oː] [aɪnə ˈhant]
Oh! A hand!

Jetzt bin ich eine Brieftaube!
[jɛtst bin iç aɪnə ˈbriːftaʊbə]
Now I am a carrier pigeon!
(lit: letter pigeon)

90

PIGEON: Ein Brief für . . . Herbert
Pappenheimer!
[aɪn 'briːf fyːr 'hɛrbɛrt 'papənhaɪmər]
A letter for . . . Herbert Pappenheimer!

Gut!
['guːt]
Good!

Ich fliege!
[iç 'fliːgə]
I (will) fly!

PIGEON COUGHS

CROWD: Tor!
['toːr]
Goal!

PIGEON: Oh!
['oː]
Oh!

PIGEON: Ein Fußball!
[aɪn ˈfuːsbal]
A soccer ball!

Post für Herbert Pappenheimer!
[ˈpɔst fyːr ˈhɛrbɛrt ˈpapənhaɪmər]
Mail for Herbert Pappenheimer!

PIGEON: Oh! Das macht nichts!

[oː] [das ˈmaxt niçts]

Oh! That doesn't matter! (lit: That makes nothing!)

"The Crazy Soccer Ball"

REFEREE: Es geht los!
[ɛs geːt ˈloːs]
Begin! (lit: It begins!)

SOCCER BALL: Ich will nicht!
[iç ˈvil niçt]
I don't want to!

SOCCER BALL: **Ich will nicht!**
[iç 'vil niçt]
I don't want to!

SOCCER PLAYER: **He! Der Ball!**
[heː] [deːr 'bal]
Hey! The ball!

Der Ball kann laufen!
[deːr 'bal kan 'laʊfən]
The ball can run!

CROWD: **Tor!**
['toːr]
Goal!

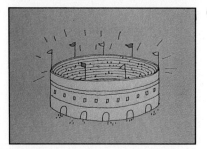

SOCCER PLAYER: Ein . . . ein Flugzeug!
[aɪn . . . aɪn ˈfluːktsɔyk]
An . . . an airplane!

CROWD: Tor!
[ˈtoːr]
Goal!

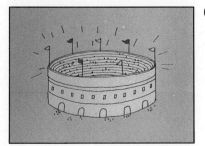

PLAYER: **Au!**
['aʊ]
Ow!

CROWD: **Tor! Tor! Bravo! Bravo!**
['toːr] ['toːr] ['brɑːvo] ['brɑːvo]
Goal! Goal! Hurrah! Hurrah!

CROWD: **Der Ball hat gewonnen!**
[deːr 'bal hat gə'vɔnən]
The ball has won!

"The Wet Organist"

MAN: Ich brauche Musik!
[iç 'braʊxə mu'ziːk]
I need music!

Ein Orgelkonzert! Ja!
[aɪn 'ɔrgəlkɔntsɛrt] [jaː]
An organ concert! Yes!

ORGAN MUSIC PLAYS, THEN BREAKS OFF

MAN: Mein Kassettenrecorder ist kaputt!
[maɪn ka'sɛtənre'kɔrdər ist ka'put]
My cassette recorder is broken!

Ich brauche Musik!
[iç 'braʊxə mu'ziːk]
I need music!

MAN: He! Das ist es!
[he:] [das ˈist ɛs]
Hey! That's it!

Ich mache selber Musik! Mit Holz!
[iç ˈmaxə ˈzɛlbər muˈzik] [mit ˈhɔlts]
I (will) make music myself! With wood!

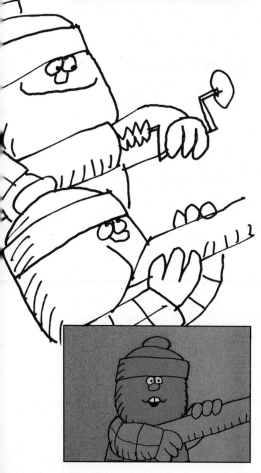

Oh! Schön!
[oː] [ˈʃøːn]
Oh! Nice!

MAN: **Fertig! Ich habe eine Orgel!**
['fɛrtiç] [iç 'haːbə 'aɪnə 'ɔrgəl]
Finished! I have an organ!

Jetzt mache ich selber Musik!
[jɛtst 'maxə iç 'zɛlbər mu'ziːk]
Now I (will) make music myself!

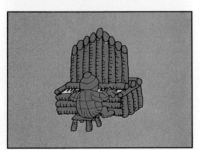

Meine Damen und Herren:
['maɪnə 'dɑmən unt 'hɛrən]
Ladies and gentlemen:

Ein Orgelkonzert!
[aɪn 'ɔrgəlkɔntsɛrt]
An organ concert!

ORGAN MUSIC

MAN: **Das ist lustig!**
[das ist ˈlʊstiç]
This is fun!

Oh! Das Wetter ist schlecht!
[oː] [das ˈvɛtər ist ʃlɛçt]
Oh! The weather is bad!

Und ich habe kein Haus!
[unt iç ˈhɑːbə kaɪn ˈhaʊs]
And I have no house!

Das macht nichts!
[das ˈmaxt niçts]
That doesn't matter!
(lit: That makes nothing!)

Ich brauche Musik!
[iç ˈbraʊxə muˈziːk]
I need music!

ORGAN MUSIC

"The Singing Pirates"

CAPTAIN:

Da! Ein Boot!
[dɑː] [aɪn ˈboːt]
There! A boat!

Wir müssen dahin!
[viːr ˈmysən daˈhin]
We must (go) there!

PIRATE:

Wohin?
[voˈhin]
Where?

CAPTAIN:

Dahin! Los!
[daˈhin] [loːs]
There! Go!

Alles fertig?
[ˈaləs ˈfɛrtiç]
Everything ready?

CREW: Ja! Fertig!
[ja:] ['fɛrtiç]
Yes! Ready!

CAPTAIN: Gut! Jetzt!
[gu:t] [jɛtst]
Good! Now!

MOTORBOAT MAN: Guten Abend, meine Herren!
[gu:tən 'ɑ:bənt 'maɪnə 'hɛrən]
Good evening, gentlemen!

CREW: **Guten Abend!**
[guːtən ˈaːbənt]
Good evening!

MOTORBOAT MAN: **Ich habe nichts!**
[iç ˈhaːbə niçts]
I have nothing!

CAPTAIN: **Nichts?**
[niçts]
Nothing?

MOTORBOAT MAN: **Nein, nichts! Ich . . .
ich kann singen!**
[naɪn ˈniçts] [iç . . . iç kan ˈziŋən]
No, nothing! I . . . I can sing!

CAPTAIN: **Singen? Ich möchte auch singen!**
[ˈziŋən] [iç mœçtə ˈaux ziŋən]
Sing? I would like to sing also!

Los! Singen!
[loːs] [ˈziŋən]
Start! Sing!

MOTORBOAT MAN SINGS

104

MOTORBOAT MAN: Und jetzt, du, singen!
[unt jɛtst 'du: 'ziŋən]
And now, you, sing!

CAPTAIN: Ich kann nicht singen!
[iç 'kan niçt ziŋən]
I cannot sing!

MOTORBOAT MAN: Du kannst! Los!
[du: 'kanst] ['lo:s]
You can! Start!

MOTORBOAT MAN, CAPTAIN & CREW SING

"The Crazy Railway Gate"

HORN

GATE LAUGHS

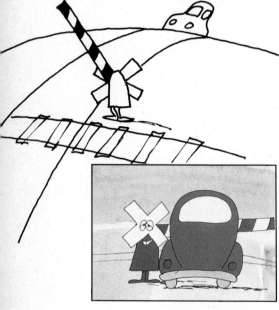

CAR: He! Aufmachen!
[he] [ˈaʊfmaxən]
Hey! Open!

GATE: Nein! Ich bin zu!
[naɪn] [iç bin ˈtsuː]
No! I am closed!

CAR: Ich will jetzt fahren!
[iç vil jɛtst ˈfaːrən]
I want to drive now!

GATE: Ich bleibe zu!
[iç blaɪbə ˈtsuː]
I am staying shut!

CAR: Aufmachen! Ich muß nach Hameln!
[ˈaʊfmaxən] [iç mus naːx ˈhaːməln]
Open! I must (go) to Hameln!

Bitte! Mach auf!
[ˈbitə] [max ˈaʊf]
Please! Open!

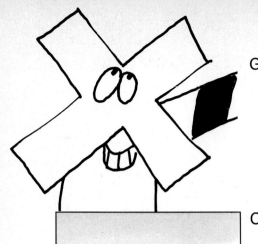

GATE: Gut! Du kannst fahren!
[guːt] [duː kanst ˈfɑːrən]
Fine! You can drive!

CAR: Au! Paß auf!
[aʊ] [pas ˈaʊf]
Ow! Watch out!

He! Was ist das?
[heː] [vas ˈist das]
Hey! What is this?

Du mußt hier weg!
[duː must hiːr ˈvɛk]
You must (go) away (from) here!

GATE: Nein! Ich bleibe!
[naɪn] [iç ˈblaɪbə]
No! I am staying (shut)!

TRAIN WHISTLE

CAR: Da! Da kommt eine Eisenbahn!
[dɑː] [dɑː kɔmt ˈaɪnə ˈaɪzenbɑːn]
There! There comes a train!

Hilfe! Ich muß hier weg!
[ˈhilfə] [iç mus hiːr ˈvɛk]
Help! I must (get) away (from) here!

GATE: Oh! Die Eisenbahn!
[oː] [diː ˈaɪzənbaːn]
Oh! The train!

CAR: Danke!
[ˈdaŋkə]
Thanks!

TRAIN: Schnell! Aufmachen!
[ʃnɛl] [ˈaʊfmaxən]
Hurry! Open!

GATE: Nein! Ich bleibe zu!
[naɪn] [iç blaɪbə ˈtsuː]
No! I am staying shut!

GATE LAUGHS

"The Little Engine"

ENGINE: He! Wann muß ich fahren?
[he:] [van mus iç 'fɑːrən]
Hey! When do I have to go?

STATION MAN: In einer Stunde!
[in 'aɪnər 'ʃtundə]
In one hour!

ENGINE: In einer Stunde!
[in 'aɪnər 'ʃtundə]
In one hour!

Ich gehe spazieren!
[iç 'geːe ʃpa'tsiːrən]
I (will) go for a walk!

STATION MAN: Was? Eine Lokomotive geht spazieren?
[vas] ['aɪnə loːkomo'tiːvə geːt ʃpa'tsiːrən]
What? An engine is going for a walk?

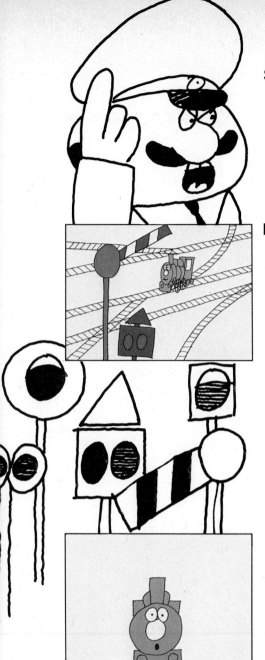

STATION MAN: Halt! Hierbleiben!
[halt] ['hi:rblaɪbən]
Stop! Stay here!

ENGINE: Oh! Wohin fahre ich jetzt?
[o:] [vo:'hin 'fɑːrə iç jɛtst]
Oh! Where do I go now?

Hierhin? Nein. Dahin? Nein.
['hi:rhin] [naɪn] ['da:hin] [naɪn]
Here? No. There? No.

Auch nicht! Wo ist der Ausgang?
[aʊx niçt] [vo: ist de:r 'aʊsgaŋ]
Not here either! (lit: Also not!)
Where is the exit?

Oh, ich muß hier weg!
[o: iç mus hi:r 'vɛk]
Oh, I have to (get) away (from) here!

Oh! Hier ist es schön!
[o:] ['hi:r ist ɛs ʃø:n]
Oh! Here it is pretty!

Hier gehe ich spazieren!
[hi:r 'ge:ə iç ʃpa'tsi:rən]
Here I (will) take a walk!

111

ENGINE: **Ich kann nicht fahren!**
[iç kan niçt ˈfɑːrən]
I cannot go (on)!

Ich brauche Kohle!
[iç ˈbrauxə ˈkoːlə]
I need coal!

MOLE: **Du brauchst Kohle? Moment!**
[duː brauxst ˈkoːlə] [moˈmɛnt]
You need coal? Just a moment!

ENGINE: **Oh! Danke!**
[oː] [ˈdaŋkə]
Oh! Thanks!

MOLE: **In fünf Minuten mußt du fahren!
Schnell!**
[in fynf miˈnuːtən must duː ˈfɑːrən] [ʃnɛl]
In five minutes you must go! Hurry!

ENGINE:

Drei Minuten . . .
[draɪ miˈnuːtən]
Three minutes . . .

Zwei Minuten . . .
[tsvaɪ miˈnuːtən]
Two minutes . . .

STATION MAN:

Eine Minute . . .
[ˈaɪnə miˈnuːtə]
One minute . . .

Abfahren!
[ˈapfɑːrən]
Depart!

Key to Pronunciation

The phonetic alphabet used in this word list is that of the Association Phonétique Internationale (A. P. I. or I. P. A. = International Phonetic Association). The length of vowels is indicated by [ː] following the vowel symbol, the stress by ['] preceding the stressed syllable. The glottal stop [|] is the forced stop between one word or syllable and a following one beginning with a stressed vowel, as in "beobachten" [bə'|obaxtən].

Sym-bol	Examples	Nearest English Equivalents	Remarks
		A. Vowels	
a	Mann [man]		short **a** as in British English "**ca**st" said quickly
ɑː	Wagen ['vɑːgən]	**fa**ther	long **a**
e	egal [e'gɑːl]	b**e**d	
eː	Weg [veːk]		unlike any English sound, though it has a resemblance to the sound in "**day**"
ə	Bitte ['bitə]	**ago**	a short sound, that of unaccented **e**
ɛ	Männer ['mɛnər] Geld [gɛlt]	**fai**r	There is no -er sound at the end. It is one pure short vowel-sound.
ɛː	wägen ['vɛːgən]		same sound, but long
i	Wind [vint]	**i**t	
iː	hier [hiːr]	m**ee**t	
ɔ	Ort [ɔrt]	l**o**ng	
o	Advokat [atvo'kɑːt]	m**o**lest [mo'lest]	
oː	Boot [boːt]		[oː] resembles the English sound in **go** [gou] but without the [u]
øː	schön [ʃøːn]		The sound may be acquired by saying [e] through closely rounded lips.
ø	Ödem [ø'deːm]		same sound, but short
œ	öffnen ['œfnən]		The sound has a resemblance to the English vowel in "**her**". Lips, however, must be well rounded as for ɔ.
u	Mutter ['mutər]	b**oo**k	
uː	Uhr [uːr]	b**oo**t	
y	Glück [glyk]		It may be acquired by saying **i** through fairly closely rounded lips.
yː	führen ['fyːrən]		same sound, but long

Symbol	Examples	Nearest English Equivalents	Remarks

B. Diphthongs

Symbol	Examples	Nearest English Equivalents	Remarks
aɪ	Mai [maɪ]	like	
aʊ	Maus [maʊs]	mouse	
ɔʏ	Beute ['bʊʏtə]	boy	
	Läufer ['lɔʏfər]		

C. Consonants

Symbol	Examples	Nearest English Equivalents	Remarks
b	besser ['bɛsər]	better	
d	du [duː]	dance	
f	finden ['findən]	find	
	Vater ['fɑːtər]		
	Photo ['foːto]		
g	Gold [gɔlt]	gold	
	Geld [gɜlt]		
ʒ	Genie [ʒe'niː]	measure	
	Journal [ʒur'nɑːl]		
h	Haus [haʊs]	house	
ç	Licht [liçt]		An approximation to this sound may be acquired by assuming the mouth configuration for [i] and emitting a strong current of breath.
	manch [manç]		
	traurig ['traʊriç]		
x	Loch [lɔx]	Scotch: loch	Whereas [ç] is pronounced at the front of the mouth, [x] is pronounced in the throat.
j	ja [jɑː]	year	
k	keck [kɛk]	kick	
	Tag [tɑːk]		
	Chronist [kro'nist]		
	Café [ka'feː]		
l	lassen [lasən]	lump	pronounced like English initial "clear l"
m	Maus [maʊs]	mouse	
n	nein [naɪn]	not	
ŋ	klingen ['kliŋən]	sing, drink	
	sinken ['ziŋkən]		
p	Paß [pas]	pass	
	Weib [vaɪp]		
	obgleich [ɔp'glaɪç]		
r	rot [roːt]	rot	There are two pronunciations: the frontal or lingual r and the uvular r (the latter unknown in English).

Symbol	Examples	Nearest English Equivalents	Remarks
s	Glas [glɑːs] Masse [ˈmasə] Mast [mast] naß [nas]	mi**ss**	unvoiced when final, doubled, or next to a voiceless consonant
z	Sohn [zoːn] Rose [ˈroːzə]	**z**ero	voiced when initial in a word or a syllable
ʃ	Schiff [ʃif] Charme [ʃarm] Spiel [ʃpiːl] Stein [ʃtaɪn]	**sh**ip	
t	Tee [teː] Thron [troːn] Stadt [ʃtat] Bad [bɑːt] Findling [ˈfintliŋ] Wind [vint]	**t**ea	
v	Vase [ˈvɑːzə] Winter [ˈvintər]	**v**ast	

Alphabetized Word Listing

A

der **Abend** (-e)
['ɑːbənt]
evening

aber
['ɑːbər]
but

abfahren
['apfɑːrən]
to depart

ach
[ax]
ah! alas!

acht
[axt]
eight

Alfred
['alfreːt]
(masculine name)

alles
['aləs]
everything

Alles Gute!
['aləs 'guːtə]
Best wishes! Good luck!

Alois
['alɔys]
(masculine name)

also
['alzoː]
so, thus

an
[an]
on

alt
[alt]
old

der **Appetit**
[ape'tiːt]
appetite

die **Arbeit** (-en)
['arbaɪt]
work, job

arbeiten
['arbaɪtən]
to work

au!
[aʊ]
ow! ouch!

aua!
['aʊa]
ow!

auch
[aʊx]
also, too

auf
[aʊf]
on

aufmachen
['aʊfmaxən]
to open

aufpassen
['aʊfpasən]
to watch out, be careful

Auf Wiedersehen!
[aʊf 'viːdərzeːən]
Good-bye!

aus
[aʊs]
off, out, from

der **Ausgang** (ᵁe)
['aʊsgaŋ]
exit

aussehen wie
['aʊszeːən viː]
to look like, have the appearance of

das **Auto** (-s)
['aʊto]
car, automobile

die **Autobahn** (-en)
['aʊtobɑːn]
freeway

B

das **Baby** (-s)
['beːbi]
baby

Bach
[bax]
(German composer)

der **Ball**
[bal]
ball

der **Bär** (-en)
[bɛːr]
bear

Barbara
['barbara]
(feminine name)

bauen
['baʊən]
to build

der **Baum** (ᵁe)
[baʊm]
tree

die **Baumspitze** (-n)
['baʊmʃpitsə]
treetop, treetop ornament

bei
[baɪ]
at, with

Bengali
[bɛŋ'gɑːli]
(masculine name)

Benjamin
['bɛnjamiːn]
(masculine name)

Berlin
[bɛr'liːn]
(German city)

besser
['bɛsər]
better

bin, bist
[bin] [bist]
see: sein

bitte
['bitə]
you're welcome, please

Bitte schön!
['bitəʃøːn]
You're welcome!

blau
[blaʊ]
blue

bleiben
['blaɪbən]
to stay, remain

bleib zu
[blaɪb tsuː]
see: zubleiben

der **Bodensee**
['boːdənzeː]
Lake Constance

das **Boot** (-e)
[boːt]
boat, ship

brauchen
['braʊxən]
to need

braun
[braʊn]
brown

Bravo!
['brɑːvo]
Bravo! Hurrah!

Bremen
['breːmən]
(German city)

der **Brief** (-e)
[briːf]
letter

die **Brieftaube** (-n)
['briːftaʊbə]
carrier pigeon, homing pigeon

das **Buch** (ᵘer)
[buːx]
book

die **Burg** (-en)
[burg]
castle

der **Bus** (-se)
[bus]
bus

die **Butter**
['butər]
butter

C

der **Christkindlmarkt** (ᵘe)
['kristkindlmarkt]
Christmas market

der **Clown** (-s)
[klaʊn]
clown

D

da
[dɑː]
there

dahin
[da'hin]
there, in that direction

die **Dame** (-n)
['dɑːmə]
lady, woman

danke
['daŋkə]
thanks, thank you

danke schön
['daŋkəʃøːn]
thank you

dann
[dan]
then

das
[das]
the, this, that, these, those

dein
[daɪn]
your, yours truly (in a letter)

dem
[deːm]
the

der
[deːr]
the

(das) **Deutschland**
['dɔytʃlant]
Germany

der **Dezember** (–)
[de'tsɛmbər]
December

dich
[diç]
you

die
[diː]
the, they, those

diese
['diːzə]
this, these

dir
[diːr]
you

doch
[dɔx]
nevertheless, however, still, yet

drei
[draɪ]
three

du
[duː]
you

E

Eduard
['eːduart]
(masculine name)

das **Ei** (-er)
[aɪ]
egg

ein
[aɪn]
a, an, one

der **Eingang** (¨e)
[ˈaɪŋgaŋ]
entrance

eins
[aɪns]
one

die **Eisenbahn** (-en)
[ˈaɪzənbaːn]
railway, railroad

Emil
[ˈeːmiːl]
(masculine name)

Emma
[ˈɛma]
(feminine name)

der **Enkel** (–)
[ˈɛŋkəl]
grandchild

er
[ɛr]
he

Erkin
[ˈeːrkiːn]
(masculine name)

es
[ɛs]
it

Es geht los!
[ɛs geːt loːs]
It begins, starts!

essen
[ˈɛsən]
to eat

etwas
[ˈɛtvas]
something

F

fahre mit
[ˈfaːrə mit]
see: mitfahren

fahren
[ˈfaːrən]
to drive, travel, go

der **Fasching**
[ˈfaʃiŋ]
carnival, Shrovetide

Felix
[ˈfeːliks]
(masculine name)

Ferdinand
[ˈfɛrdinant]
(masculine name)

fertig
[ˈfɛrtiç]
finished, ready

das **Feuer** (–)
[ˈfɔyər]
fire

der **Feuerschlucker** (–)
[ˈfɔyərʃlukər]
fire eater

der **Fisch** (-e)
[fiʃ]
fish

die **Flasche** (-n)
[ˈflaʃə]
bottle

die **Flaschenorgel** (-n)
[ˈflaʃənɔrgəl]
bottle-organ

das **Flaschenschiff** (-e)
[ˈflaʃənʃif]
ship in a bottle

fliegen
[ˈfliːgən]
to fly

das **Floß** (¨e)
[floːs]
raft

die **Flöte** (-n)
[ˈfløːtə]
flute

der **Flugkapitän** (-e)
[ˈfluːkkapitɛːn]
aircraft captain, pilot

der **Flugplatz** (¨e)
[ˈfluːkplats]
airport, airfield

das **Flugzeug** (-e)
[ˈfluːktsɔyk]
airplane

das **Foto** (-s)
[ˈfoːto]
photograph

Frankfurt am Main
[ˈfraŋkfurt am maɪn]
*Frankfurt on the Main
(German city)*

Franz
[frants]
(masculine name)

die **Frau** (-en)
[fraʊ]
woman, wife, Mrs.

der **Freund** (-e)
[frɔynt]
friend

frisch
[friʃ]
fresh

fröhlich
[ˈfrøːliç]
merry, happy, joyful

das **Frühstück** (-e)
[ˈfryːʃtyk]
breakfast

fünf
[fynf]
five

für
[fyːr]
for

der **Fuß** (¨e)
[fuːs]
foot

der **Fußball** (¨e)
[ˈfuːsbal]
soccer, soccer ball

G

der **Geburtstag** (-e)
[gə'buːrtstaːk]
birthday

gehen
['geːən]
to go

gehe spazieren
['geːə ʃpa'tsiːrən]
see: spazierengehen

geht los
[geːt loːs]
see: losgehen

geht's
[geːts]
see: Wie geht's?

die **Gelben**
['gɛlbən]
the yellow ones (team)

gemacht
[gə'maxt]
done, made

die **Geographie**
[geogra'fiː]
geography

gern
[gɛrn]
gladly

geschlossen
[gə'ʃlɔsən]
closed

die **Gesundheit**
[gə'zunthaɪt]
health

Gesundheit!
[gə'zunthaɪt]
Bless you!

gewonnen
[gə'vɔnən]
won

Gisela
['giːzɛlə]
(feminine name)

die **Gitarre** (-n)
[gi'tarə]
guitar

das **Glas** (⸚er)
[glaːs]
glass

das **Glück**
[glyk]
luck, happiness

Glück auf!
[glyk 'aʊf]
Good luck! (miner's greeting)

gratulieren
[gratu'liːrən]
to congratulate

groß
[groːs]
big

größte, am größten
['grøːstə, am 'grøːsten]
biggest, the biggest

grün
[gryːn]
green

gucken
['gukən]
to look

gut
[guːt]
good, fine, well

das **Gute** (-n)
['guːtə]
the good (part or thing)

Guten Abend!
[guːtən 'aːbənt]
Good evening!

Gute Nacht!
[guːtə 'naxt]
Good night!

Guten Appetit!
[guːtən ape'tiːt]
Bon appétit!

Guten Morgen!
[guːtən 'mɔrgən]
Good morning!

Guten Tag!
[guːtən 'taːk]
Good day!

H

das **Haar** (-e)
[haːr]
hair

haben
['haːbən]
to have

hallo
[ha'loː]
hello

halten
['haltən]
to stop

Hameln
['haːməln]
(German city)

die **Hand** (⸚e)
[hant]
hand

Hans
[hans]
(masculine name)

der **Harz**
[haːrts]
Harz Montains

hat
[hat]
see: haben

hatschi
[ha'tʃiː]
ah-choo (sneeze)

das **Haus** (⸚er)
[haʊs]
house

He!
[heː]
Hey!

Heinrich
['haɪnriç]
(masculine name)

heiß
[haɪs]
hot

heißen
['haɪsən]
to be called

121

helfen
['hɛlfən]
to help

her
[heːr]
here

Herbert
['hɛrbɛrt]
(masculine name)

Hermann
['hɛrman]
(masculine name)

der **Herr** (-en)
[hɛr]
man, gentleman, Mr.

Herr Ober
[hɛr 'oːbər]
waiter

heute
['hɔytə]
today

hier
[hiːr]
here

hierbleiben
['hiːrblaɪbən]
to stay here

hierher
['hiːrheːr]
here, this way, over here

hierhin
['hiːrhin]
here, in this direction

die **Hilfe** (-n)
['hɪlfə]
help

Hilfe!
['hɪlfə]
Help!

der **Himmel** (–)
['hɪməl]
sky, heavens, heaven

hinterher
[hintər'heːr]
behind, in the rear

hinterherfliegen
[hintər'heːrfliːgən]
to fly behind, follow

das **Holz** (ᵉer)
[hɔlts]
wood

hören
['høːrən]
to hear

Hubert
['huːbɛrt]
(masculine name)

der **Hund** (-e)
[hunt]
dog

hundert
['hundərt]
hundred

der **Hunger**
['huŋər]
hunger

I

ich
[iç]
I

ihr
[iːr]
you (informal plural)

im
[im]
see: in dem

in
[in]
in, into

ins
[ins]
see: in das

Irene
[i'reːnə]
(feminine name)

ist
[ist]
see: sein

J

ja
[jɑː]
yes

jetzt
[jɛtst]
now

Josef
['joːzɛf]
(masculine name)

Juchuu!
[jux'hʊ]
Whoopee! Bravo!

K

der **Kaffee** (-s)
['kafe]
coffee

die **Kaffeemaschine** (-n)
['kafema'ʃiːnə]
coffee machine

der **Kakao** (-s)
[ka'kɑːo]
cocoa

kalt
[kalt]
cold

kann, kannst
[kan, kanst]
see: können

der **Kapitän** (-e)
[kapi'tɛːn]
captain

kaputt
[ka'put]
broken

die **Kassette** (-n)
[ka'sɛtə]
cassette tape

der **Kassettenrecorder** (–)
[ka'sɛtənre'kɔrdər]
cassette recorder

kein
[kaɪn]
not a, not any, no

der **Kilometer** (–)
['ki:lome:tər]
kilometer

das **Kind** (-er)
[kint]
child, kid

der **Kinderzirkus**
['kindər'tsirkus]
children's circus

klein
[klain]
small, little

die **Kohle** (-n)
['ko:lə]
coal

Köln
[kœln]
Cologne (German city)

komisch
['ko:miʃ]
funny, comical, strange

kommen
['kɔmən]
to come

komm mit
[kɔm 'mit]
see: mitkommen

der **Kompaß** (-sse)
['kɔmpas]
compass

können
['kœnən]
to be able to, can

das **Konzert** (-e)
[kɔn'tsɛrt]
concert

kosten
['kɔstən]
to cost

das **Krankenhaus** (¨er)
['kraŋkənhaus]
hospital

die **Kuh** (¨e)
[ku:]
cow

L

lang
[laŋ]
long

laufen
['laufən]
to run, walk

laufe Ski
['laufə 'ʃi:]
see: skilaufen

das **Leben** (–)
['le:bən]
life

der **Lebkuchen** (–)
['le:pku:xən]
gingerbread

das **Licht** (-er)
[liçt]
light

die **Limonade** (-n)
[limo'na:də]
soft drink, fruit juice

links
[liŋks]
left, to the left

Lise
['li:zə]
(feminine name)

die **Lokomotive** (-n)
[lokomo'ti:və]
locomotive, engine

los
[lo:s]
up, go, start, going on

losgehen
['lo:sge:ən]
to start, begin

lustig
['lustiç]
fun, pleasing

M

mach auf
[max 'auf]
see: aufmachen

mache mit
[maxə 'mit]
see: mitmachen

machen
['maxən]
to make, do

macht nichts
['maxt 'niçts]
doesn't matter, never mind (lit: makes nothing)

der **Main**
[main]
(German river)

mal
[ma:l]
once (intensifier, as in guckt mal*)*

die **Mama** (-s)
[ma'ma]
Mama

der **Mann** (¨er)
[man]
man

die **Mark** (–)
[mark]
mark (German money)

die **Marmelade** (-n)
[marmə'la:də]
jam, marmalade

Martin
['marti:n]
(masculine name)

die **Maschine** (-n)
[ma'ʃi:nə]
machine

die **Maus** (¨e)
[maus]
mouse

Max
[maks]
(masculine name)

mein
[main]
my

der **Meter** (–)
['me:tər]
meter

mich
[mɪç]
me

die Milch
[mɪlç]
milk

der Minirecorder (–)
[ˈminireˈkɔrdər]
mini cassette recorder

die Minute (-n)
[miˈnuːtə]
minute

mir
[miːr]
me

mit
[mit]
with, along

mitfahren
[ˈmitfɑːrən]
to drive, go with

mitkommen
[ˈmitkɔmən]
to come, go along with

mitmachen
[ˈmitmaxən]
to cooperate, go along with, take part in

möchten
[ˈmœçtən]
to desire, wish, would like

der Moment (-e)
[moˈmɛnt]
moment

Moment!
Wait a moment!
Just a moment!

der Monat (-e)
[ˈmoːnat]
month

Monika
[ˈmoːnika]
(feminine name)

der Morgen (–)
[ˈmɔrgən]
morning

der Motor (-en)
[ˈmoːtɔr]
engine, motor

Muh!
[muː]
Moo!

München
[ˈmynçən]
Munich (German city)

das Museum (-een)
[muˈzeːum]
museum

die Musik
[muˈziːk]
music

muß, mußt
[mus, must]
see: müssen

müssen
[ˈmysən]
to have to, must

die Mutter (⸚)
[ˈmutər]
mother

N

na
[na]
well

nach
[nɑːx]
to, towards

nach Hause
[nɑːx haʊsə]
home

nach oben
[nɑːx ˈoːbən]
to the top

die Nacht (⸚e)
[naxt]
night

nach unten
[nɑːx ˈuntən]
to the bottom

nehmen
[ˈneːmən]
to take

nein
[naɪn]
no

neun
[nɔyn]
nine

nicht
[niçt]
not

nichts
[niçts]
nothing

nochmal
[ˈnɔxmɑːl]
again, one more time

der Norden
[ˈnɔrdən]
north

die Nordsee
[ˈnɔrtzeː]
North Sea

der November (–)
[noˈvɛmbər]
November

die Nudel (-n)
[ˈnuːdəl]
noodle

null
[nul]
zero

die Nummer (-n)
[ˈnumər]
number

nun
[nuːn]
well

Nürnberg
[ˈnyrnbɛrk]
Nuremberg (German city)

O

oben
[ˈoːbən]
at the top, above

oder
['oːdər]
or

oh!
[oː]
oh!

oje!
[o'jeː]
oh my!

der **Onkel** (–)
['ɔŋkəl]
uncle

der **Opa** (-s)
['oːpa]
grandpa

die **Orgel** (-n)
['ɔrgəl]
organ

das **Orgelkonzert** (-e)
['ɔrgəlkɔn'tsɛrt]
organ concert

Oskar
['ɔskar]
(masculine name)

P

der **Papa** (-s)
[pa'pɑː, 'papa]
Papa

Pappenheimer
['papənhaɪmər]
(surname)

paß auf
[pas 'auf]
see: aufpassen

Paul
[paʊl]
(masculine name)

Paula
['paʊla]
(feminine name)

Pauline
[paʊ'liːnə]
(feminine name)

Paulus
['paʊlus]
(masculine name)

die **Pause** (-n)
['paʊzə]
break

Peter
['peːtər]
(masculine name)

der **Pfarrer** (–)
['pfarər]
minister, pastor

der **Pfennig** (-e)
['pfɛniç]
penny (1/100th of a German mark)

die **Post**
[pɔst]
mail

die **Puppe** (-n)
['pupə]
doll

R

der **Rattenfänger** (–)
['ratənfɛŋər]
rat catcher

rechts
[rɛçts]
right, to the right

der **Recorder** (–)
[re'kɔrdər]
cassette recorder

der **Rhein**
[rain]
Rhine (German river)

der **Rheinstein**
['reinʃtaɪn]
(German castle on the Rhine river)

der **Ritter** (–)
['ritər]
knight

der **Roboter** (–)
['roːbɔtər]
robot

rot
[roːt]
red

die **Ruhe**
['ruːə]
quiet, silence

S

der **Salat** (-e)
[za'lɑt]
salad, lettuce

das **Salz** (-e)
[zalts]
salt

das **Schaf** (-e)
[ʃɑːf]
sheep

das **Schiff** (-e)
[ʃif]
ship

schlafen
['ʃlɑːfən]
to sleep

schlecht
[ʃlɛçt]
bad, terrible

der **Schluß** (¨sse)
[ʃlus]
end, close

der **Schnee**
[ʃneː]
snow

der **Schneemann** (¨er)
['ʃneːman]
snowman

schnell
[ʃnɛl]
fast, quickly, hurry

schneller
['ʃnɛlər]
faster

schön
[ʃøːn]
beautiful, nice, pretty

schönste, am schönsten
['ʃøːnstə, am 'ʃøːnstən]
*most beautiful, the most
beautiful*

die Schule (-n)
['ʃuːlə]
school

Sebastian
[ze'bastian]
(masculine name)

sechs
[zɛks]
six

der See (-n)
[zeː]
lake

die See (-n)
[zeː]
sea, ocean

der Seehund (-e)
['zeːhunt]
seal

sehen
['zeːən]
to see

sehr
[zeːr]
very, much

sein
[zaɪn]
to be

selber
['zɛlbər]
see: selbst

selbst
[zɛlpst]
self, oneself

selig
['zeːliç]
blessed

sie
[ziː]
she, they

Sie
[ziː]
you (formal)

sieben
['ziːbən]
seven

Siegfried
['ziːgfriːd]
(masculine name)

sieht aus
[ziːt 'aʊs]
see: aussehen

sind
[zint]
see: sein

singen
['ziŋən]
to sing

der Ski (-er)
[ʃiː]
ski

das Skifahren
['ʃiː faːrən]
skiing

skifahren
['ʃiː faːrən]
to ski

das Skilaufen
['ʃiː laʊfən]
skiing

skilaufen
['ʃiː laʊfən]
to ski

der Skiopa (-s)
['ʃiː oːpa]
skiing grandpa

die Skischule (-n)
['ʃiːʃuːlə]
ski school

so
[zoː]
so, well, such, that

der Sohn (ᵘe)
[zoːn]
son

spät
[ʃpɛːt]
late

spazierengehen
[ʃpaˈtsiːrəngeːən]
to take a walk, go for a walk

das Spiel (-e)
[ʃpiːl]
game, play

spielen
['ʃpiːlən]
to play

die Spitze (-n)
['ʃpitsə]
top, treetop, treetop ornament

Stephanie
['ʃtɛfani]
(feminine name)

der Stern (-e)
[ʃtɛrn]
star

stoppen
['ʃtɔpən]
to stop

die Stunde (-n)
['ʃtundə]
hour

Susanne
[zuˈzanə]
(feminine name)

T

der Tag (-e)
[taːk]
day

die Tante (-en)
['tantə]
aunt

die Taube (-n)
['taʊbə]
pigeon

das Taxi (-s)
['taksi]
taxi, cab

der Tee (-s)
[teː]
tea

das **Telefon** (-e)
[tele'foːn]
telephone

teuer
['tɔyər]
expensive

Thomas
['toːmas]
(masculine name)

die **Tochter** (ᵁ)
['tɔxtər]
daughter

das **Tor** (-e)
[toːr]
goal

der **Tourist** (-en)
[tu'rist]
tourist

das **Training**
['trɛːnɪŋ]
training

tschuff, tschuff
[tʃuf]
chug, chug

tschüs
[tʃys]
good-bye

die **Tuba** (-ben)
['tuːba]
tuba

tun
[tuːn]
to do

U

die **U-Bahn** (-en)
['uːbaːn]
subway

die **Uhr** (-en)
[uːr]
clock, watch; o'clock

Ulrich
['ulrɪç]
masculine name)

um
[um]
around, at

und
[unt]
and

unser
['unzər]
our

unten
['untən]
below, under, down

V

der **Vater** (ᵁ)
['faːtər]
father

(der) **Vati** (-s)
['faːti]
daddy

verboten
[fɛr'boːtən]
forbidden

Veronika
[ve'roːnika]
(feminine name)

viel
[fiːl]
much, a lot

vier
[fiːr]
four

von
[fɔn]
from, of, belonging to

Vorsicht
['foːrzɪçt]
careful!

W

wann
[van]
when

warum
[va'rum]
why

was
[vas]
what, something

was für ein
[vas fyːr aɪn]
what kind of a

das **Wasser** (–)
['vasər]
water

weg
[vɛk]
gone, away

weggehen
['vɛkgeːən]
to go away

(die) **Weihnachten**
['vaɪnaxtən]
Christmas

der **Weihnachtsbaum** (ᵁe)
['vaɪnaxtsbaʊm]
Christmas tree

die **Weihnachtsbaumspitze** (-n)
['vaɪnaxtsbaʊmʃpitsə]
Christmas treetop ornament

der **Weihnachtsmann** (ᵁer)
['vaɪnaxtsman]
Santa Claus

die **Weihnachtsmaus** (ᵁe)
['vaɪnaxtsmaʊs]
Christmas mouse

weiß
[vaɪs]
see: wissen

weiß
[vaɪs]
white

wer
[veːr]
who

die **Weser**
['veːzər]
(German river)

der **Westen**
[vestən]
west

das **Wetter**
['vɛtər]
weather

wie
[viː]
how, like, as

Wiedersehen!
['viːdərzeːən]
see: Auf Wiedersehen!

Wie geht's?
[viː geːts]
How are you? (lit: How goes it?)

wieso
[vi:'zoː]
why, why so, but why

Wilhelm
['vilhɛlm]
(masculine name)

will, willst
[vil, vilst]
see: wollen

Willi
['vili]
(masculine name)

wir
[viːr]
we

wissen
['visən]
to know

wo
[voː]
where

wohin
[vo:'hin]
where (. . . to)

Wolfsburg
['vɔlfsburk]
(German city)

die **Wolke** (-n)
['vɔlkə]
cloud

wollen
['vɔlən]
to want

das **Würstchen** (–)
['vyrstçən]
sausage

Z

zehn
[tseːn]
ten

der **Zirkus** (-se)
['tsirkus]
circus

der **Zoo** (-s)
[tsoː]
zoo

zu
[tsuː]
to, too, closed

zubleiben
['tsuːblaɪbən]
to stay, remain shut

der **Zucker**
['tsukər]
sugar

zu Hause
[tsu 'hauzə]
at home

zum
[tsum]
see: zu dem

zumachen
['tsumaxən]
to close, shut

zuviel
[tsu'fiːl]
too much

zwei
[tsvaɪ]
two